DUST TO EAT

DUST TO EAT

Drought and Depression in the 1930s

MICHAEL L. COOPER

Clarion Books
New York

To Doc and Rozina Thomas,
benevolent hosts of sailing adventures,
beach excursions, long dinners, and good conversations

Clarion Books
a Houghton Mifflin Company imprint
215 Park Avenue South, New York, NY 10003
Copyright © 2004 by Michael L. Cooper

Quotations from *Letters from the Dust Bowl,* by Caroline Henderson,
copyright © 2001 by the University of Oklahoma Press, Norman, Okla.
Reprinted by permission of the publisher.

Lyrics on page 9 are from "Do Re Mi." Words and music by Woodie Guthrie. TRO-© copyright 1961
(renewed) 1963 (renewed) Ludlow Music, Inc., New York, N.Y. Used by permission. Lyrics on pages
12 and 37 are from "Dust Storm Disaster." Words and music by Woodie Guthrie. TRO-© copyright
1960 (renewed) 1963 (renewed) Ludlow Music, Inc., New York, N.Y. Used by permission.

Maps by Kayley LeFaiver.
The text was set in 12-point Meridien.

For information about permission to reproduce selections from this book,
write to Permissions, Houghton Mifflin Company,
215 Park Avenue South, New York, NY 10003.
www.houghtonmifflinbooks.com

Printed in the U.S.A.

Library of Congress Cataloging-in-Publication Data

Cooper, Michael L., 1950-
Dust to eat : drought and depression in the 1930s / by Michael L. Cooper.
p. cm.
Includes bibliographical references and index.
ISBN 0-618-15449-3
1. United States—History—1919–1933—Juvenile literature. 2. United States—
History—1933–1945—Juvenile literature. 3. Depressions—1929—United States—
Juvenile literature. 4. Droughts—Great Plains—History—20th century—Juvenile literature.
5. Dust storms—Great Plains—History—20th century—Juvenile literature. 6. Migrant labor—
California—History—20th century—Juvenile literature. 7. New Deal, 1933–1939—Juvenile
literature. [1. United States—History—1919–1933. 2. United States—History—1933–1945.
3. Depressions—1929. 4. Droughts—Great Plains. 5. Dust storms—Great Plains.] I. Title.
E806.C63 2004   973.917—dc22   2003017807

KPT   10   9   8   7   6   5   4   3   2   1

ACKNOWLEDGMENTS

Special thanks to Alvin O. Turner, the editor of Caroline Henderson's letters, for providing the photograph of Caroline and Will Henderson. I'm also indebted to the Hendersons' daughter, Dr. Eleanor Grandstaff, and their grandson, David Grandstaff, for generously sharing their memories. And many thanks to Charlie Gable, a middle school social studies teacher, who keeps me abreast of the reading interests of twelve-year-olds.

Contents

MAP OF THE DUST BOWL   viii

INTRODUCTION   x

1 THE "OKIE" PROBLEM   1

2 THE DIRTY THIRTIES   11

3 "DUST TO EAT, DUST TO BREATHE, DUST TO DRINK"   23

4 CALIFORNIA-BOUND   37

5 HARVEST GYPSIES   47

6 CRISIS IN THE VALLEY   57

7 WORLD WAR II ENDS THE DEPRESSION   65

SOURCE NOTES   71

OF FURTHER INTEREST   75

INDEX   77

INTRODUCTION

"It is good to remember that the laws of the universe recognize no favorites and cherish no hostility or small vindictiveness; that before sun and rain, stormy winds, or summer's kind benefi- cence, we all stand upon one common level."

—Caroline Henderson

It is tempting to think of the Great Depression and the Dust Bowl disaster as ancient history. But these dual disasters of the 1930s shaped the country we live in today. Together, they created more hardship and suffering than any other event in our national past except the Civil War. Like that bloody conflict, the depression decade was a turning point in American history.

The economic crisis known as the Great Depression began in 1929 and lasted ten years. It caused widespread unemployment, poverty, and despair that affected nearly every man, woman, and child. As if that were not trouble enough, just a few years after the depression began came the Dust Bowl. It was an environ- mental disaster caused, in part, by a long, severe drought that turned a vast region of farm and ranch land to desert.

The Great Depression and the Dust Bowl forced millions of people to leave their homes. Those events also left tens of thousands of men, women, and children without adequate shelter or food. They survived as best they could, living in old automobiles, in boxcars, or on the streets.

Before the depression decade, Americans had few "safety nets." There were no federal unemployment, retirement, or welfare programs to help people who had fallen on hard times. Americans had long believed in limited or laissez-faire government. But the depression and the Dust Bowl made people understand that misfortune can happen to anyone. It also made them realize that the federal government could play an important role in protecting the jobs, homes, and health of its citizens. But that lesson was learned only after a long, painful crisis.

The enduring work of two Californians have helped us remember the 1930s. One was novelist John Steinbeck. His novel *The Grapes of Wrath,* about an Oklahoma family who become migrant farm workers, is among the most widely read books of all time. The second was Dorothea Lange, who captured the despair and deprivation of those years in thousands of black-and-white photographs, some of which are reproduced in this book.

1

THE "OKIE" PROBLEM

"Thousands of them are crossing the borders in ancient rattling automobiles, destitute and hungry and homeless, ready to accept any pay so that they may eat and feed their children," John Steinbeck wrote in a 1936 article for the *San Francisco News*.

An editor at the *News* had asked the writer, who was already well known for two novels about California's migrant workers, *In Dubious Battle* and *Tortilla Flat*, to investigate the plight of a new breed of migrants streaming into California's San Joaquin Valley. Steinbeck knew that these people were fleeing farms and small towns in the Great Plains and southwestern states, where the Dust Bowl and the Great Depression had made life impossible.

In August 1936, Steinbeck packed an old bakery van, which he had nicknamed "the Pie Wagon," with a cot, blankets, cooking utensils, and an ice chest. He drove the makeshift camper from his home in Los Gatos, a small town near San Jose, east into the San Joaquin Valley and then south nearly 200 miles.

An "ancient rattling automobile," like those John Steinbeck saw in the San Joaquin Valley. DOROTHEA LANGE/LIBRARY OF CONGRESS

John Steinbeck, the author of
The Grapes of Wrath.
NATIONAL ARCHIVES

Steinbeck first stopped at the Arvin Sanitary Camp, near the city of Bakersfield. This camp, which the residents called "Weedpatch," was the first of more than a dozen camps that the Farm Security Administration, a new federal agency, set up to temporarily house homeless migrants. He met the camp manager, Tom Collins, and the two men quickly became friends. In his conversations with Collins, Steinbeck learned that an estimated 150,000 men, women, and children had recently moved into the valley. They hoped to earn two or three dollars a day picking fruits and vegetables.

Before Steinbeck left Weedpatch, another official warned him to be careful. The valley's powerful ranch owners, or growers, were trying to stop the migrant workers from joining unions.

Local thugs and policemen, believed to be working for the growers, had beaten and jailed union members. The growers were suspicious of any stranger who appeared to be sympathetic to the plight of the workers.

Steinbeck quietly visited a number of squatter camps, which the valley's permanent residents disdainfully called "Little Oklahomas" or "Okievilles." Homeless migrants had settled in dozens of communities of makeshift dwellings near highways and irrigation ditches. He wrote that a typical camp looked like a garbage dump. "You can see a litter of dirty rags and scrap iron, of houses built of weeds, of flattened cans or of paper."

At one camp, Steinbeck visited several families. The only furniture in one tiny shack was a soggy mattress lying on the dirt floor.

Tom Collins with residents of the Arvin Sanitary Camp.
DOROTHEA LANGE/LIBRARY OF CONGRESS

An Okieville, where residents built shacks out of discarded lumber, cardboard boxes, and old cars. DOROTHEA LANGE/LIBRARY OF CONGRESS

The mother and father, thin Midwesterners, spoke softly, while their four dirty children stared silently at the visitor. The family could not afford furniture, clothing, or even soap, the father said, because they needed all their money for food. He felt lucky because other camp residents were penniless, and some had been forced to eat rats and dogs.

In front of another shack, Steinbeck saw a boy, about three years old, wearing only a burlap feed sack. The child's stomach had swollen up like a balloon from malnutrition. "He sits on the ground in the sun in front of the house and the little black fruit flies buzz in circles and land on his closed eyes and crawl up his nose until he weakly brushes them away." The author predicted that the boy would soon die. Many migrant children already had.

Steinbeck was not the only one to write about the squalid conditions. One journalist found "a two-room cabin in which forty-one people from southeastern Oklahoma were living." A *Los Angeles Times* reporter told his readers that "a visit to these squatter camps leaves one aghast."

After nearly two weeks of visiting and talking with people in the San Joaquin Valley, Steinbeck returned home to write his articles. Along the way, he stopped in Salinas, the town where he had grown up. There he saw some of the violence he had been warned about earlier.

Cabbage pickers, led by men who were trying to organize a

Homeless migrants living behind a billboard. DOROTHEA LANGE/LIBRARY OF CONGRESS

union, were on strike. To combat the strikers, growers and businessmen had persuaded a retired army general to take charge of the local police and the court. The general had declared martial law in the town. He organized his own militia of shopkeepers and salesmen, armed them with ax handles, and sent them to patrol the streets. They seized men suspected of being union leaders and locked them up. The declaration of martial law, the makeshift militia, and the confinement of union organizers were all illegal, but no one challenged the general. It was, a historian later said, "one of the most flagrant vigilante actions in California history."

Back home in Los Gatos, Steinbeck felt shaken by what he had witnessed. "I just returned from the strike area of Salinas, and from my migrants in Bakersfield," he wrote to a friend. "This thing is dangerous. Maybe it will be patched up for a while, but I look for the lid to blow off in a few weeks." However, unlike earlier strikes by agricultural workers, the Salinas strike did not turn violent.

Other Californians, especially the residents of the farming towns, did not share Steinbeck's sympathy for the migrant families. They called them such names as "tin-can tourists," "Arkies," "Texicans," "dust bowlers," "hillbillies," "harvest gypsies," "squatters," and "fruit tramps." But the most common name was "Okies." This was a slang word for people from Oklahoma. But only some of the people called Okies were actually from Oklahoma; more came from other states, such as Kansas and Texas. But Californians just lumped all of the poor newcomers together. "No matter where you come from," said a Missouri man, "you're an Okie when you get to California."

Few valley residents had a kind word for the migrants. Okies

A destitute family in Marysville, California. The father explained that he had been a cotton farmer. He had earned $7,000 in Texas in 1927, but he went broke in 1931 and lost his farm. DOROTHEA LANGE/LIBRARY OF CONGRESS

were "shiftless trash who live like hogs, no matter how much is done for them," complained a Bakersfield doctor. They're "ignorant filthy people," a businessman said, who should not "think they're as good as the next man."

The state's leading farm journal, *Pacific Rural Press,* joined the chorus of condemnation. "Migrants mean trouble in many ways," stated an editorial. They "add to our unemployment, our relief burden, and our disease and crime troubles. . . . The crime record of these migrants includes a lot of sordid, depraved acts."

Californians tried to stop poor people from moving into their state. One group rented a billboard on Route 66 near Tulsa, Oklahoma. The large sign beside the most traveled highway to southern California warned:

NO JOBS IN CALIFORNIA
IF YOU ARE LOOKING FOR WORK—KEEP OUT
6 MEN FOR EVERY JOB
NO STATE RELIEF AVAILABLE FOR NON-RESIDENTS

The Los Angles chief of police, James E. Davis, sent 125 policemen to the state's eastern and northern borders in January 1936 to establish checkpoints on the main highways. Newspapers called them "bum blockades." It was illegal for city policemen to use their authority outside Los Angeles, but few Californians objected. For six months, the officers stopped cars of migrants and turned away the poorest—frequently those with less than fifty dollars.

The bum blockades inspired one of the many songs about poor people that Woody Guthrie, a young Oklahoma musician who traveled to California in 1936, wrote:

Migrants came from many states. These children were from Kansas, Nebraska, South Dakota, California, and Missouri. LIBRARY OF CONGRESS

Oh, if you ain't got the do re mi, folks, if you ain't got the do re mi,
Why, you better go back to beautiful Texas,
Oklahoma, Kansas, Georgia, Tennessee.
California is a garden of Eden,
A paradise to live in or see,
But believe it or not you won't find it so hot, if you ain't got the do re mi.

But no matter how much they tried, Californians could not stop the flow of poor people.

A storm descends on a town. LIBRARY OF CONGRESS

2

THE DIRTY THIRTIES

In 1934, the nation began to realize that something was terribly wrong on the Great Plains. On May 9, a dust storm carried an estimated 350 million tons of dirt two thousand miles eastward. Weathermen calculated that four million tons of prairie dirt fell on Chicago—four pounds for each city resident. The following day, the dust darkened the sky over Buffalo, New York, and Atlanta, Georgia. Three hundred miles out into the Atlantic Ocean, brown prairie dirt fell like snow on the decks of ships.

People still talk about "the Great Dust Storm of 1935." Lila Lee King and a friend were playing at home in Liberal, Kansas, on Sunday, April 14, when they saw a towering wall of black clouds rushing across the prairie toward the town.

"I was sure I was going to die," Lila told an interviewer decades later, "and I can vividly recall the dust storm, although I was only eleven at the time."

Woody Guthrie was living that year in Pampa, a northwest

Texas town a hundred miles south of Liberal, when the storm struck. "A whole bunch of us was standing just outside of town," the folk singer recalled in his autobiography, *Bound for Glory.* "We watched the dust storm come up like the Red Sea closing in on the Israel children. It got so black when that thing hit we all run into the house." A few hours later he wrote the song "The Great Dust Storm."

> *It fell across the city*
> *Like a curtain of black rolled down*
> *We thought it was our judgment*
> *We thought it was our doom.*

A news story the following day by Associated Press reporter Robert Geiger gave the stricken region its name: "Three little words, achingly familiar on a Western farmer's tongue, rule life in the dust bowl of the continent—if it rains." After his story appeared in newspapers, people began calling the parched region the Dust Bowl.

Years of hot weather, drought, and excessive farming caused the Great Dust Bowl disaster. A shortage of rain and scorching temperatures baked the nation in the mid-1930s. *Newsweek* magazine described the country as "a vast simmering cauldron." Summer temperatures in 1934 topped 120 degrees Fahrenheit in Iowa and 115 in Nebraska, and remained above 100 degrees for weeks in Illinois. To escape the heat, the magazine reported, one man climbed into his refrigerator; he stayed there so long he had to be taken to the hospital and treated for frostbite.

The drought and the dust often made headlines. LIBRARY OF CONGRESS

Neither drought nor dust storms were unusual on the Great Plains, but no one alive had ever seen drought or dust as severe as they were in the 1930s. The Great Plains is a broad swath of prairie that stretches across thirteen states, from the Rocky Mountains east to the Mississippi Valley, from southern Texas up through North Dakota and far into Canada. Crops withered and died; rivers and wells ran dry; the soil hardened and cracked. The winds that regularly sweep across the prairie gathered the dry dirt and carried it away, creating dust storms that people living on the plains called "black blizzards."

The drought and blowing sand turned 150,000 square miles of farm and ranch land into "a picture of complete destruction, one of the most serious peacetime problems in the nation's

A black blizzard looming over Elkhart, Kansas. LIBRARY OF CONGRESS

history," said Rexford Tugwell, director of the Resettlement Administration.

It was difficult to locate the Dust Bowl precisely on a map. One year, the drought and dust were worst in South Dakota. The next, they were worst in Kansas. And the year after that, New Mexico was suffering the most. The heart of the Dust Bowl turned out to be southern Kansas, western Oklahoma, northern Texas, northeastern New Mexico, and southeastern Colorado.

Oddly enough, the prosperity of previous years had helped cause the Dust Bowl disaster—and the Great Depression as well.

The federal government had encouraged farmers during World War I to grow as much wheat as possible. "Plant more wheat. Wheat will win the war!" urged one government slogan. "If you can't fight, farm!" advised another. The government even guaranteed farmers $2 for every bushel. Wheat prices more than doubled, from $.93 to $2.30 a bushel. American wheat farmers prospered.

After World War I ended in 1918, the war-torn European nations struggled for years to recover from the devastation. Meanwhile, they bought food from the United States. Wheat prices remained high in the 1920s, encouraging farmers to eagerly buy up as much land as they could afford, or purchase on credit, in order to plant more of the grain. Historians call this hectic period of the 1920s "the Great Plow Up."

New technology—mainly the tractor and the disk harrow—made the Great Plow Up possible. In 1915, only a few thousand tractors tilled the soil in states like Oklahoma. Just ten years later, farmers in Oklahoma alone owned over fifty thousand tractors. Then the disk harrow replaced the old single-blade iron plow. The long row of circular blades on the new plow easily chopped through the tough prairie grass that anchored the soil.

With their new machinery, plains farmers were able to work long into the night sowing wheat. Some planted crops right up to the front doors of their homes. By the end of the 1920s, farmers were growing three times more wheat than they had grown at the beginning of the decade. Wheat was the most important crop on the Great Plains. But the prairie had lost eleven million

Good weather produced bumper wheat crops in the 1920s.

acres of the tough native grasses that, for centuries, had held the earth in place during the region's frequent droughts and windstorms.

Farmers were not the only Americans on a buying spree that decade. Their city cousins were purchasing new cars, houses, and radios. To meet the skyrocketing demand for goods, businesses invested heavily in factories, machinery, and warehouses. Banks made borrowing money easy. Buying on time—paying in installments, which is so common today—became popular in the 1920s.

Americans believed prosperity had become a permanent part of national life. Observers dubbed that lively and prosperous decade "the Roaring Twenties."

This optimism encouraged more people to invest money in the stock market. Major stocks doubled in value between 1928 and the middle of 1929. Investors imagined that they had found an easy way to become wealthy. The stock market became a national obsession.

Late in the decade, banks raised interest rates. The higher rates abruptly curbed borrowing and spending—silencing the Roaring Twenties.

In October 1929, stock prices fell sharply, the first big decline in nearly two years. So many people panicked and dumped their stocks that on October 29 the market crashed. Observers called that day "Black Tuesday." In the last days of October, the market

A fleet of Ford tractors, called Fordsons, on a Texas ranch. LIBRARY OF CONGRESS

lost half of its value, some $16 billion. The decline continued into November.

The decade's prosperity had caused people to become intoxicated. When the good times ended, the hangover was huge. Sales of cars, tractors, houses, and other goods plunged.

It was an odd circle. Americans became unemployed because there were no jobs. There were no jobs because consumers could not afford to buy goods. And people could not afford to buy goods because they were unemployed.

By 1932, one in every four workers was jobless. Unemployment soared even higher in some industrial cities. In Cleveland, Ohio, half of all workers lost their jobs, while in Toledo, Ohio, four out of every five adults were jobless. Suddenly, starving and homeless people were everywhere, sleeping in parks, in doorways, under bridges, and in sewer pipes. They dug through garbage cans looking for old bread, half-eaten apples, or chicken bones. City hospitals reported an alarming increase in deaths from starvation.

The worst of the depression spread to the Great Plains with the beginning of the new decade. In the fall of 1931, farmers had harvested so much wheat that they ran short of storage space. But they were in for a shock when they trucked their grain to market. There was so much wheat for sale that the price had dropped to just pennies a bushel. Farmers on the plains would not have another good crop for ten years.

The following winter the weather turned unusually bad. "Four freight cars on our new railway went hurtling along the track for about forty miles, set in motion and carried forward solely by the violence of the wind and their own momentum," observed

Unemployed men in Chicago line up for free coffee and doughnuts. NATIONAL ARCHIVES

Caroline Henderson. Caroline and her husband, Will, were farmers in western Oklahoma. They owned a 960-acre farm, where they grew wheat and raised cattle. Caroline wrote a series of magazine articles for *The Atlantic Monthly* describing day-to-day life during the difficult years of the Dust Bowl and depression.

The strong wind that sent 20-ton freight cars speeding down the railroad tracks, Caroline later realized, was the beginning "of a long continued series of violent wind and dust storms that turned this plains country into a veritable desert."

The storms, Caroline said, not only would lay waste to the land but would also create hardship for all of the prairie's inhabitants. "On our bleak Easter morning a jack rabbit sat crouched in the

An abandoned tenant house in the middle of a newly plowed field.
DOROTHEA LANGE/LIBRARY OF CONGRESS

The drought and dust killed tens of thousands of animals. LIBRARY OF CONGRESS

kindling pile by the kitchen door. He was, however no frolicsome Easter bunny, but a starved, trembling creature with one eye battered out by the terrific dust storms of the preceding week.

"When these wild creatures, ordinarily so well able to take care for themselves, come seeking protection, their necessity indicates a cruel crisis for man and beast."

A midday dust storm in Amarillo, Texas, forces drivers to turn on their headlights.
ARTHUR ROTHSTEIN/LIBRARY OF CONGRESS

3

"Dust to Eat, Dust to Breathe, Dust to Drink"

On the Great Plains, people lived with both economic depression and with dust. It was possible, at times, to forget the depression. But it was impossible to forget the dust.

"Today we went to Texhoma and were dismayed to find ourselves out in another of the raging dust storms which have made life miserable here for so long," said Caroline Henderson, describing a car trip with her husband to the town eighteen miles south of their farm. "We hoped they were over; but they were turning on lights in all of the stores by 1:30. We left town about 2:00 and had to creep along burning our lights all the way home. Often we could hardly see the length of the car ahead of us through the clouds of pulverized soil."

Black blizzards in the winter and spring darkened the plains nearly every week. Some blew over within an hour or two, while

An automobile, a wagon, and farm equipment nearly buried by dust in Dallas, South Dakota. NATIONAL ARCHIVES

others lingered three or four days. In Amarillo, a city in north Texas, black blizzards in 1935 caused complete blackouts for a total of 908 hours, over a month of darkness.

The blizzards came up quickly, trapping people outdoors and in their cars and aboard trains. Some people died. One seven-year-old Kansas boy wandered away from home during a storm. When the air cleared, his parents found him suffocated in a mound of sand. The strong winds in Kansas swept another little boy several hundred yards from his house. Searchers found him tangled up in a barbed-wire fence, cut and bruised but alive.

Each big storm left victims choking and spitting up clods of dirt. They rushed to their local hospitals. But the only treatment was to rinse the mud out of their mouths with water, swab the dirt from their nostrils with Vaseline, and wash the grit from their eyes with boric acid. Babies, the elderly, and people with existing lung problems such as asthma suffered the most. Some caught "dust pneumonia," gasping for breath for weeks or months before recovering—or dying.

Plains residents tried all sorts of ways to avoid breathing the deadly dirt. Some sealed the windows in their homes with tape or oil-soaked cloths. Others slept with damp washcloths over their noses and mouths. A few wore World War I–era gas masks, which

A boy tries to avoid breathing the dust.
ARTHUR ROTHSTEIN/
LIBRARY OF CONGRESS

made them look a little like space aliens. After each storm, people tried to clear the air in their houses by flapping wet towels. But there was no way to avoid the dust completely. It seeped into everything.

"At the little country store," Caroline Henderson reported, "after one of the worst of these storms, the candies in the show case all looked alike and equally brown. Dust to eat and dust to breathe and dust to drink. Dust in the beds and in the flour bin, on dishes and walls and windows, in hair and eyes and ears and teeth and throats. . . ."

The constant dust made farm work much harder. "There were

A black blizzard sweeps across the Colorado prairie. LIBRARY OF CONGRESS

*Caroline and Will Henderson
as newlyweds on their
Oklahoma homestead.*
COURTESY OF DR. ELEANOR
GRANDSTAFF

many days, as I struggled to care for the stock," she continued, "when I could not see from one of the farm buildings to another through the blinding, choking clouds. Dust was piling up everywhere, filling gateways, burying machinery, drifting around the buildings, making the less traveled roads almost impassable. The mere matter of getting milk or even water to the house in a condition fit for use presented a difficult problem."

The devastation resulting from drought and dust was visible everywhere by 1934. "We saw many pitiful reminders of broken hopes and apparently wasted effort," Caroline noted after a trip

Sand dunes nearly cover farm buildings. ARTHUR ROTHSTEIN/LIBRARY OF CONGRESS

to the nearby town of Guymon. "Little abandoned homes now walled in or half buried by banks of drifted soil . . . a painful story of loss and disappointment."

Families unable to raise crops or livestock could not repay the money they had borrowed to buy tractors and land during earlier, more prosperous years. All around her, Caroline saw that "land once owned and occupied by farm families is now passing into ownership of banks, mortgage companies, assurance societies, and investment partnerships or corporations."

When a bank takes possession of property because the owner fails to repay a mortgage or loan, it is called "foreclosure." Foreclosures were a major problem across the nation during the Great Depression. One-third of all farms were lost to foreclosure.

Caroline described the plight of one neighbor who lost his farm. "Troubles in his family, some years of short crops, and the low prices of the past three seasons have broken him. He has lost his 960 acres of land and most of his stock. He is now trying desperately, and I think without much chance of success, to get a government loan to buy back a few of his cattle and start all over again—old, half-blind, almost barehanded—in a Texas valley."

Some of Caroline's other neighbors were in even worse straits. "We spent Thanksgiving Day trying to help a sorely afflicted family. Five of the children were down at once with typhoid fever in a family who had already lost their stock, truck, car, tractor, and

An orchard ruined by drought and dust. ARTHUR ROTHSTEIN/LIBRARY OF CONGRESS

some say their farm. One boy had already died and two girls since, with two young men still very low."

She also described an incident that might have been funny except it showed how desperately poor people had become. "Out here we thought the depths of the Depression had been fathomed some time ago, when the sheriff subtracted from the very personal possessions of one of our neighbors a set of false teeth that he had been unable to pay for."

People in the small towns in the Dust Bowl suffered along with the farmers. When farm income in Cimarron County, at the western tip of the Oklahoma panhandle, plunged from $1.2 million in

Empty buildings in the town of Caddo, Oklahoma.
DOROTHEA LANGE/LIBRARY OF CONGRESS

One of many Kansas farms for sale. LIBRARY OF CONGRESS

1931 to only $7,000 in 1933, the loss crippled businesses in the county seat of Guymon. Two of the town's three banks closed. (Some nine thousand banks throughout the country closed during the Great Depression.) The shelves in grocery stores stayed bare, except for dust. And schoolteachers went month after month without pay. Nearly half of the people in the town and surrounding county had to move away.

Many farmers and merchants moved to Denver, Oklahoma City, or other cities in the region. But life in depression-era cities was difficult, too. Roy Turner told an interviewer that he, his wife, and their young children had lived over a year in a squatter camp of two thousand residents next to the Oklahoma City stock-yards. They had built a shack from pieces of junked cars, cardboard boxes, and "just anything that we could get to build one out of." They did not like the smell and noise from the herds of cattle awaiting slaughter, but at least his hungry family could sneak into the stockyards to milk the cows.

Families made homeless by the depression and the dust storms had few places where they could turn for help. Programs that exist today, such as unemployment insurance and public housing, did not exist in the early 1930s. A few states had small welfare funds, but the huge number of needy people quickly drained them of money.

Many Americans pinned their hopes for better times on a new president. They gave Franklin D. Roosevelt, whose campaign slogan promised "a new deal for America," a landslide victory over the incumbent, Herbert Hoover, in the election of 1932. Roosevelt took office in 1933, and his administration immediately set to work to try to end the depression through a series of programs and policies known as "the New Deal."

In a feverish period called "the First Hundred Days," the new president sent Congress numerous pieces of legislation to help factories, banks, farms, and unemployed people. Two new laws that especially helped farmers were the Works Progress Administration (WPA) and the Agricultural Adjustment Act (AAA).

The WPA hired out-of-work farmers and factory workers to build schools, pave dirt roads, and put up bridges.

The AAA, starting with $134 million in 1934, paid farmers to reduce the amount of wheat and other crops they grew in order

President Franklin D. Roosevelt signing legislation during the First Hundred Days. With him is Secretary of the Treasury William H. Woodin.
LIBRARY OF CONGRESS

to end the glut of farm products on the market. With fewer farm products for sale, prices would go up. The AAA proved to be one of the more successful of the New Deal programs. By 1936, farm prices had risen by 50 percent.

"Like most people here we signed the contracts for wheat acreage reduction, taking out 39 acres for 1934." Caroline explained how the federal programs helped her and others in her county: "Businessmen as well as the farmers themselves realize that the benefit payments under AAA and the wage payments

A poster advertising the Works Progress Administration.
VERA BROCK, ARTIST/LIBRARY OF CONGRESS

from federal work projects are all that have saved a large territory here from abandonment."

But AAA programs had the unforeseen effect of hurting some families. Over half of all farmers at the beginning of the 1930s were tenants or sharecroppers. Many of them worked on cotton plantations. When AAA payments reduced cotton growing by half in states such as Texas and Oklahoma, landowners no longer needed as many sharecroppers, tenants, and farm hands.

"In '34, I had I reckon four renters and I didn't make anything," said one Oklahoma farm owner. "I bought tractors on the money the government give me and got shed [rid] of my renters. You'll find it everywhere all over the country that way. They got their choice—California or WPA."

The WPA could not employ every jobless worker. In the plains states alone, some three million people left their farms in the 1930s. They had to go where they could find jobs. For many that meant California.

Migrants stopping beside the highway for lunch. DOROTHEA LANGE/LIBRARY OF CONGRESS

4

CALIFORNIA-BOUND

We loaded our jalopies
And piled our families in,
We rattled down that highway
To never come back again.

— Woody Guthrie

Unlike the early pioneers who went west looking for land, the migrants of the 1930s were fleeing drought, dust storms, and hunger. They were refugees who had been "burned out, blown out, and starved out."

California was the most popular destination. *Business Week* magazine observed in 1937 that the state was experiencing "one of the greatest inter-state migrations since the gold rush." Many migrants headed to the San Joaquin Valley after seeing handbills distributed by labor agents or after receiving letters from relatives or friends reporting that the valley's ranches needed workers.

Hard-pressed Americans imagined California to be a kind of paradise, where life would be easy. Migrants composed songs and poems about what they expected to find. Soon after arriving in the San Joaquin Valley from the Southwest, Flora Robertson expressed her hopes in a poem called "Why We Come to California."

California, California,
here I come too.
With a coffee pot and skillet,
and I'm coming to you.
Nothing's left in Oklahoma,
for us to eat or do.
And if apples, nuts, and oranges,
and Santa Claus is real,
Come on to California,
eat and eat till you're full.

Migrants traveled to the big state in different ways. The poorest walked, hitchhiked, or hopped freight trains. One Kansas woman told her mother about seeing a couple on Thanksgiving "footing it along the highway, dragging a little wagon and two small children."

Woody Guthrie tried hitchhiking from Pampa to California. He spent several days on Route 66, getting only short rides with farmers and truck drivers. It was winter, cold and snowy. In New Mexico, after several hours of walking, he decided to hop a freight train. Thousands of jobless men illegally rode freight trains back and forth across the country. Woody hopped a freight and

Oklahoma sharecroppers, too poor to own a car, looking for work and a place to live. DOROTHEA LANGE/LIBRARY OF CONGRESS

found himself in a boxcar with several other men, and they all huddled together for warmth.

Unlike Guthrie, some migrants traveling to California could afford a train or bus ticket. Others paid a few dollars to ride in a neighbor's automobile or truck. But most drove.

A young man hopping a freight train in Bakersfield, California.
LIBRARY OF CONGRESS

Many migrants owned Model T cars purchased in the prosperous 1920s, when they cost less than $300 each. People called them "farmers' cars" because engineers had designed the high chassis for travel over unpaved country roads. Used cars were even cheaper. One Oklahoma couple bound for California in 1935 bought an eight-year-old Chevrolet Roadster for only $7.50.

It was easy to spot the cars on Route 66 that belonged to migrant families. They were crammed full of people, baggage, and furniture. The father drove, his wife sat quietly beside him, and three or four children filled the back seat. Boxes, chairs, washtubs—even mattresses—were strapped to the sides and tops of the cars. For about $10 worth of gas (gasoline in those days cost only a few pennies a gallon), migrants from as far east as Arkansas could complete the trip to California in three or four days. Along the way, some spent the nights in auto courts, the forerunners of modern motels. Others, wanting to save their money, camped beside the highway and cooked potatoes, beans, and bologna over open fires. The trip was an easy one for most travelers.

Jewell and Gladys Morris were teenagers when their father decided to move the family to California. He loaded as much clothing and furniture as possible in a cattle trailer, hitched it to the family's ten-year-old car, and drove off. The sisters had never been away from home. They enjoyed camping and cooking outdoors. The girls felt as though they were on vacation. But not everyone had such a pleasant journey.

Flossie Haggard and her husband, Jim, made the trip from Oklahoma. "In July, 1935, we loaded some necessary supplies onto a two wheel trailer and our 1926 model Chevrolet which Jim had overhauled. We headed for California on Route 66, as many friends and relatives had already done. We had our groceries with us—home sugar cured bacon in a lard can, potatoes, canned vegetables, and fruit. We camped at night and I cooked in a Dutch oven. The only place we didn't sleep out was in Albuquerque [New Mexico] where we took a cabin and where I can remember bathing."

A family of nine from Arkansas is packed into this automobile.
LIBRARY OF CONGRESS

Highway 58, the road many migrants traveled over the Tehachapi Mountains and into the San Joaquin Valley. Library of Congress

   Once the Haggards crossed the California state line and entered the Mojave Desert, their car broke down. Daytime temperatures in the desert can exceed 120 degrees Fahrenheit. "We were out of water, and just when I thought we weren't going to make it," Flossie said, "I saw this boy coming down the highway on a

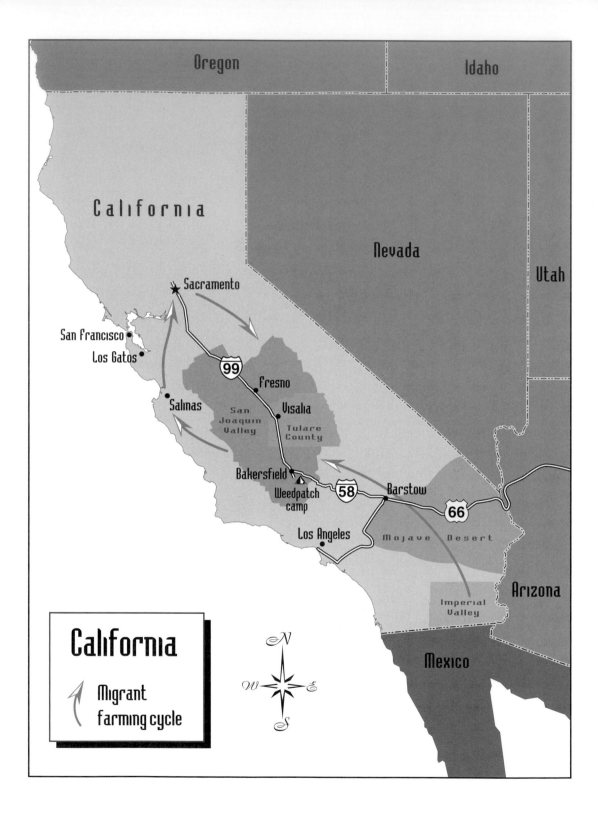

bicycle. He was going all the way from Kentucky to Fresno. He shared a quart of water with us and helped us fix the car. Everybody's been treating us like trash, and I told this boy, 'I'm glad to see there's still some decent folks left in this world.'"

The Morrises, the Haggards, and anyone else bound for the San Joaquin Valley left Route 66 at Barstow, continuing westward on Highway 58. The old cars struggling under their heavy loads crawled up the two-lane road on the eastern slope of the Tehachapi Mountains to nearly four thousand feet above sea level and then sailed down the western slope into the flat San Joaquin Valley. For many migrants, the trip to California proved easier than the life they found there.

A migrant family's car, broken down in the California desert.
DOROTHEA LANGE/LIBRARY OF CONGRESS

A girl going to the cotton fields at 7 A.M. Many migrant children worked alongside their parents. DOROTHEA LANGE/LIBRARY OF CONGRESS

5

Harvest Gypsies

The San Joaquin Valley is one of the world's most productive farming regions.

Central California's dry, hot summers and extensive irrigation ditches supplying water from the mountains enable the valley's ranchers to grow more than two hundred different crops, including potatoes, grapes, sorghum, figs, oranges, plums, olives, hay, tomatoes, peaches, rice, beans, and asparagus. Today machines gather many of the vegetables and fruits, but growers in the 1930s depended on an army of some 200,000 people to pick the crops and pack them in boxes for shipment across the nation.

The valley's residents were used to seeing migrants on the roads and in the fields at harvest time. Many of the pickers were Filipino, Chinese, or Japanese. Once, the largest number of laborers had been Mexican. Thousands of men and women from Mexico used to journey north to harvest crops for half a year and then return home. This annual custom stopped in 1929, when a new immigration law went into effect restricting the number of foreign-born people allowed to enter the United States. Soon afterward, as unemployment rose in the early years of the depression, federal and state authorities forced a half million Mexican citizens living in the southwestern states to return to Mexico.

To replace the Mexican workers, Californians advertised in newspapers and distributed leaflets in the Dust Bowl states, where there were so many out-of-work farmers. By 1936, the advertisements, along with simple word of mouth, had encouraged nearly a

A sign for cotton pickers, in Spanish and English, near Fresno, California.
Dorothea Lange/Library of Congress

Harvest gypsies on their way up Highway 99 to the next crop.
DOROTHEA LANGE/LIBRARY OF CONGRESS

quarter of a million migrants to move to the San Joaquin Valley, where they joined the army of laborers in the annual harvest.

The pickers followed a thousand-mile circuit of maturing fruits and vegetables. They began in the spring in the Imperial Valley, near the Mexican border, picking early crops such as peas and strawberries. A few weeks later, the migrant families packed up their old cars and raced north to work in the San Joaquin Valley. Next, they rushed over to the Salinas Valley, and then up to the Sacramento Valley. Finally, in early autumn the migrants returned south to the San Joaquin Valley to harvest cotton and hay. The families hurried from valley to valley, crop to crop, because there were more workers in each area than were needed. The first people to arrive got the jobs.

Gang labor: Mexicans and whites harvest carrots for the eastern market.
DOROTHEA LANGE/LIBRARY OF CONGRESS

The work was not easy. "I had never tried that before," said a man from Kansas who had been picking cotton. "And you sure could tell it when I got out there because I picked about eighty pounds that first day and I worked hard all day long. I finally got so that I could pick about three hundred pounds, but you can't make any money out of that at a cent a pound."

The newcomers often had difficulties with unfamiliar crops, such as asparagus. To harvest these tender green shoots, pickers spent hours squatting between the long rows of low plants. The growers fired people who were unable to work fast.

During the harvest season, workers rented tents or houses on the ranches where they worked. In one of his articles, Steinbeck described the typical migrant houses: "one-room shacks usually about 10 by 12 feet, have no rug, no water, no bed. In one corner there is a little iron wood stove. Water must be carried from the faucet at the end of the street." Growers charged workers as much as $2 a day for one of these houses.

Children of the migrant workers changed schools six or seven times in a single year. Many of them stopped going to school alto-

The "main street" of a migrant camp in Farmington, California.
DOROTHEA LANGE/LIBRARY OF CONGRESS

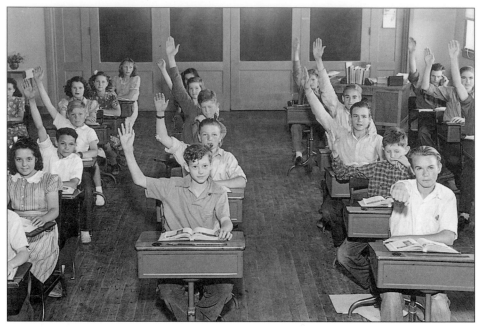

A class of seventh and eighth graders in Stanislaus County. The kids with their hands raised all moved to California during the 1930s.
DOROTHEA LANGE/LIBRARY OF CONGRESS

gether. "The better dressed children shout and jeer," one parent told Steinbeck. "The teachers are quite often impatient with these additions to their duties, and the parents of the 'nice' children do not want to have disease carriers in the schools."

Wayne Rogers's family moved to California from the Southwest when he was a child. He recalled that "the school nurse used to check us for lice. And as she looked through our hair and our ears, she would tell us, 'Okies have lice.' That really made me feel terrible."

Because of their poor diets and unsanitary living conditions,

The community barber at work. DOROTHEA LANGE/LIBRARY OF CONGRESS

A boy in the Tulare FSA camp in Visalia, California.
ARTHUR ROTHSTEIN/
LIBRARY OF CONGRESS

many migrants became sick. One county reported six thousand cases of influenza, or flu, in February 1937. Migrant children in Tulare County died at a rate of two a day. A major problem was their poor diet. Many of them ate only beans, potatoes, bread, oatmeal, and dandelion greens. There was no milk or protein.

The work was hard, the pay low, and the living conditions bad. Yet for many newcomers it was a better life than the one they

A large family from Oklahoma in Brawley, California.
DOROTHEA LANGE/LIBRARY OF CONGRESS

had left behind. "I left there and come to California to try to support my family and to school it," said Bill Robinson, who traveled from Oklahoma with his wife and six children. "And I'm proud to come and don't have any intention of going back, 'cause I can make a living here so much easier than I could there."

But it became much harder to make a living as the number of poor migrants increased rapidly in 1936 and 1937.

A migrant camp in February 1936. DOROTHEA LANGE/LIBRARY OF CONGRESS

6

CRISIS IN THE VALLEY

"I must go to Visalia. Four thousand families, drowned out of their tents, are really starving to death," John Steinbeck told his literary agent, Elizabeth Otis, in the winter of 1938.

A crisis in the San Joaquin Valley, near Visalia, some thirty miles southeast of Fresno, had been building since summer. It started when growers advertised for twenty-five thousand workers for the autumn cotton harvest. Nearly three times that number responded. There were not enough jobs for everyone, and many people were left with no money and nowhere to go.

Harold Robinson, an official with the Salvation Army, reported that he had seen families "seeking shelter and subsistence in the fields and woods like wild animals."

The federal Farm Security Administration supplied food and water to the stranded migrants. It was just enough aid to avoid mass starvation, but nothing more. That winter, the coldest and wettest in memory for many Californians, was a season of suffering for thousands of homeless families.

A family fashioned a makeshift shelter out of canvas and their car.
DOROTHEA LANGE/LIBRARY OF CONGRESS

Steinbeck stocked the Pie Wagon with supplies and picked up his friend Tom Collins. The two men drove to Visalia.

"When we reached the flooded areas we found John's old pie truck useless, so we set out on foot," Collins later wrote. "For forty-eight hours, and without food or sleep, we worked among the sick and the half-starved people, dragging some from under trees to a different sort of shelter, dragging others from torn and ragged tents, flooded with water, stagnant water, to the questionable shelter of a higher piece of ground."

The tragedy greatly disturbed Steinbeck. "It is the most heart-breaking thing in the world," the author wrote when he was back at his typewriter in Los Gatos. "The death of children by starvation in our valleys is simply staggering." The sight of so many desperate people and his anger at local officials for not providing more aid inspired Steinbeck to begin work on what he called his "big book."

But the crisis evoked little sympathy from other Californians. Rather, it seemed to increase prejudice against the Okies.

"No greater invasion by the destitute has ever been recorded in the history of mankind," said Thomas W. MacManus, a Bakersfield businessman. He wanted "California jobs to go to Californi-

A destitute mother with four of her seven children and their few possessions.
DOROTHEA LANGE/LIBRARY OF CONGRESS

Two families from Missouri discussing where to look for work.
Dorothea Lange/Library of Congress

ans and not to the horde of empty bellies from the Southwest who come in answer to the tribal call, 'There's food in California.'" MacManus was the secretary of the California Citizens Association. Businessmen and growers in Bakersfield created the association in June 1938 to try to force poor migrants to leave the state.

The association circulated a petition that called for the federal government to "aid and encourage the return of the idle thousands now here to their respective states." School children went door-to-door asking their neighbors to sign the petition. When 100,000 Californians had signed it, the association sent the peti-

13 TO 22   SAN FRANCISCO, SATURDAY, APRIL 1, 1939

ACTION ON THE MIGRANT PROBLEM

California's Representatives Study President's
Report on State Conditions; All Agreed
Solution Must Be on National Basis

BY RUTH FINNEY
The News Washington Correspondent

WASHINGTON, April 1.—During the two weeks President
Roosevelt is at Warm Springs, Ga., members of the Cali-

N FRANCISCO EXAMINER: MONDAY, FEBRUARY 27, 1939

Squalor in Tent Cities

Congress

State Faces Crisis in Caring for Migrants

Idle Hordes Offer Fertile

Migrants

U. S. to Speed Relief

WASHINGTON, March 29 — Office of Education and the

F. R. Acts To Relieve Migrants

**Orders Establishment
Of Special Body to
Cope With Problem**

WASHINGTON, Feb. 19 —
Acting on authorization given
by President Roosevelt before

OLSON PROMISES TO VETO BILL PROHIBITING POOR FROM COMING INTO STATE

Governor Says American Citizens Have Constitutional Right to Travel Anywhere; Treats

BAR MIGRANTS WITH DISEASES, COUNTIES URGE

Northern Supervisors Send
'Medical Passport' System
to Congress

By United Press

UBA CITY, Feb. 25.—Supervis-
of the Alta California Area of
northern counties adopted a reso-
lion today urging Congress to sup-
t a bill designed to forbid en-
nce to California of indigent mi-
nts carrying "contaminating dis-

BATTLE TO CURB MIGRANT INVASION

Citizens Organize Against Horde's Influx

CCCC   THE SAN FRANCISCO EXAMINER: THURSDAY, MARCH 7

Communists' Conquest Over Migrants Stirs Californians

Okies' Camp

VOTE GROWS

ASSOCIATED FARMERS ANSWER

Reply to Dispatch on Committee

100 Cotton Strikers Jailed at Bakersfield

The San Francisco News

15 TO 26   SAN FRANCISCO, MONDAY, MAY 23, 1938   Pag

LEAN TIME AHEAD FOR MIGRANTS

Numerous California newspaper headlines reflected the migrants' problems.

LIBRARY OF CONGRESS

A billboard advertising the movie version of The Grapes of Wrath. *Migrants lived in the tents behind the billboard.* DOROTHEA LANGE/LIBRARY OF CONGRESS

tion to the U.S. Congress. However, the congressmen did little with the petition other than appoint a committee to investigate California's migrant problem.

Other people raised their voices against the newcomers. California state legislators in 1933 passed the Indigent Act, which made it a crime to bring indigent, or poor, people into the state. County prosecutors did not enforce the law until five years later, when they convicted more than twenty migrants for bringing their relatives into the state.

The legislators tried to abolish the State Relief Administration, because they claimed migrants moved to California only to collect state relief checks, which averaged about $40 a month for a family of four. "If they come to this state, let them starve or stay away," growled Republican State Senator William Rich. The legislators did not close the agency, but they did replace the one-year residency requirement with a three-year residency requirement. This change cut the number of people receiving relief checks by half.

In Los Gatos, Steinbeck paid little attention to the state legislature. He was too busy writing day and night. In just six months he finished a manuscript of over 600 pages. Carol Steinbeck, editing and retyping her husband's work before sending it to the publisher, gave the manuscript its title: *The Grapes of Wrath*. Viking Press published the novel in early 1939. The following year it won the Pulitzer Prize for fiction. That same year the Hollywood director John Ford brought out a movie based on the novel.

The Grapes of Wrath was indeed John Steinbeck's "big book." It made the author famous and wealthy. And it left an enduring account of the hardships created by the Dust Bowl and the Great Depression. But the novel did little to improve the plight of the Okies. It took another crisis to do that.

Soldiers march up Fifth Avenue in New York City. LIBRARY OF CONGRESS

7

WORLD WAR II ENDS THE DEPRESSION

On December 7, 1941, when the Japanese bombed Pearl Harbor, Californians began worrying less about homeless Okies and more about possible spies among the state's eighty thousand Japanese American residents.

The United States went to war, and World War II ended the depression. The four-year fight against Japan and Germany created 17 million new jobs, making everything from uniforms and blankets to ships and airplanes. Some 15 million men and women joined the army, navy, and marines. There were more jobs than workers. Millions of women filled occupations traditionally held by men, such as welder and heavy-equipment operator. In cities like Washington, D.C., the average family income doubled between 1938 and 1942.

Many of the people who had migrated to the San Joaquin Valley in the 1930s worked their way out of the fields and orchards. They became carpenters, construction workers, truck drivers, and

People going to work in a warplane factory. LIBRARY OF CONGRESS

gas station owners. Their children learned trades or attended college to become teachers, accountants, and engineers.

On the Great Plains, rain returned in 1941 and ended the long drought. The Dust Bowl became a bad memory, as Caroline and Will Henderson and other wheat farmers once again planted their crops.

With war stories filling the newspapers, few people noticed how much America had changed during the 1930s. There were some visible symbols of that change. Young men in the Civilian Conservation Corps, another New Deal program created to put unemployed people to work, planted a long row of more than two hundred million trees—cottonwood and willow, hackberry and cedar, Russian olive and Osage orange—stretching all the way from North Dakota to the panhandle of north Texas. They called this wall of trees the Shelter Belt. As the trees grew, they helped tame the prairie wind and keep the soil from blowing away.

The Shelter Belt was just one of several conservation programs inspired by the Dust Bowl. The Roosevelt administration created the Soil Conservation Service to teach farmers new techniques of tilling their fields. "The saving of the broken lands," *Fortune* mag-

Men and women building B-17 bombers. ANDREAS FEININGER/LIBRARY OF CONGRESS

Rain returned to the Great Plains and ended the drought. LIBRARY OF CONGRESS

azine predicted, "will stand out as the great and most enduring achievement of the time."

The WPA was among the most visible and successful New Deal programs. It employed over 8.5 million jobless farmers, factory workers, students, and artists. Many of these people would have been homeless or in California picking vegetables if not for WPA jobs. In just eight years, WPA workers built or renovated 125,110 schools, post offices, and other public buildings; constructed 600 airports; paved 651,087 miles of roads; built or repaired 124,031 bridges and 8,192 parks.

The Great Depression and Dust Bowl encouraged numerous new laws and regulations to protect the environment, safeguard people's investments, and give workers a minimum wage and safe working conditions. They helped farmers sell their crops at fair prices and enabled families to have homes.

The biggest legislative achievement of the depression decade was the Social Security Act of 1935. Social Security gave many old people retirement incomes. It also initiated a much broader goal of creating programs to protect all citizens against a wide range of calamities, such as poverty, homelessness, disability, and ill health.

Conservative critics complained that the Social Security Act violated traditional values of individualism and self-help. Liberal critics called the act unfair because it did not cover agricultural laborers, or maids, cooks, and other domestic workers, most of whom were African American, Mexican, or other people of color. But Social Security immediately proved popular with the majority of Americans. Today, we all are much safer from hunger and homelessness than our great-grandparents were in the early twentieth century.

The Great Depression and the Dust Bowl made Americans understand that their national government could be an important force protecting them from both natural and man-made disasters. No one ever again wanted to see the suffering that John Steinbeck and so many other people witnessed in the 1930s.

A government poster promoting tree planting and soil conservation.
JOSEPH DUSEK, ARTIST/LIBRARY OF CONGRESS

Source Notes

1: The "Okie" Problem

Much of this chapter is based on John Steinbeck's *The Harvest Gypsies* (Berkeley, Calif.: Heyday Books, 2002), a reprint of three long newspaper articles about the migrants that he wrote for the *San Francisco News* in 1936. For information about the author's life, I relied on Jackson J. Benson's *The True Adventures of John Steinbeck, Writer* (New York: Viking Penguin, 1984) Most of the information about how California residents responded to the migrants comes from James N. Gregory's *American Exodus: The Dust Bowl Migration and Okie Culture in California* (New York: Oxford University Press, 1989). Woody Guthrie is another person closely identified with the hard times of the 1930s. I used, and enjoyed, Elizabeth Partridge's acclaimed biography, *This Land Was Made for You and Me: The Life and Songs of Woody Guthrie* (New York: Viking, 2002). I also dipped into Guthrie's autobiography, *Bound for Glory* (New York: Dutton, 1943), for its firsthand accounts of dust storms and hobo life.

2: The Dirty Thirties

Donald Worster's *Dust Bowl: The Southern Plains in the 1930s* (New York: Oxford University Press, 1979) inspired my interest in the Dust Bowl. This slim book, which makes a dry topic fascinating, is a model of historical writing that exposes the cultural roots that grew into the Dust Bowl disaster. I was fortunate to find Caroline Henderson's *Letters from the Dust Bowl* (Norman, Okla.: University of Oklahoma Press, 2001), a collection of letters edited by Alvin O. Turner. Caroline Henderson was an excellent writer, and her letters and magazine articles are a fascinating description of an Oklahoma homestead and of the changes that transformed farm life in the 1920s and 1930s. For facts and general information about the depression and the Dust Bowl, I relied on Alan Brinkley's *American History* (New York: McGraw-Hill, 1991) and on *The Reader's Companion to American History,* edited by Eric Foner and John A. Garraty (Boston: Houghton Mifflin, 1991).

3: "Dust to Eat, Dust to Breathe, Dust to Drink"
With their book, *An American Exodus* (New Haven: Yale University Press, 1969), Dorothea Lange and her husband, Paul Schuster Taylor, probably did more than anyone other than Steinbeck to publicize the plight of the Dust Bowl migrants. Some sources credit Taylor, who was an economist at Berkeley, for first bringing the plight of the migrants to widespread attention. Good firsthand accounts are found in Henderson's *Letters from the Dust Bowl* and in the first chapter of Worster's *Dust Bowl.*

4: California-Bound
Gregory's *American Exodus* supplied many of the migrants' travel stories as well as their poems. Guthrie's *Bound for Glory* describes his hitchhiking trips, a common way for boys and men to travel about the country during the depression. The first part of Dan Morgan's *Rising in the West: The True Story of an "Okie" Family from the Great Depression Through the Reagan Years* (New York: Knopf, 1992) also provided useful firsthand information about the California migrants. The poem "Why We Come to

California" is from the Charles Todd and Robert Sonkin Migrant Recordings, August 27, 1941, Visalia, California, in the Archive of Folk Culture, Library of Congress.

5: HARVEST GYPSIES

Gregory's *American Exodus* gives a good description of California's agricultural business. I got a sense of the San Joaquin Valley's dimensions from "A Geographer Looks at the San Joaquin Valley" by James J. Parsons. The article is a reprint of the 1987 Carl Sauer Memorial Lecture at the University of California, Berkeley. It can be found at http://geography.berkeley.edu/ProjectsResources/Publications/Parsons_SauerLect.html. Parsons is the source of the surprising fact that the San Joaquin Valley is one of the richest agricultural regions in the history of the world. Gregory also mentions this in *American Exodus.*

6: CRISIS IN THE VALLEY

Most of this chapter is based on Steinbeck's *The Harvest Gypsies; The True Adventures of John Steinbeck, Writer;* and *Steinbeck: A Life in Letters,* edited by Elaine Steinbeck and Robert Wallsten (New York: Viking, 1975), a book that will interest the author's devoted fans. Gregory's *American Exodus* provided most of the details about the California Citizens Association and other antimigrant groups.

7: WORLD WAR II ENDS THE DEPRESSION

The facts and figures in this chapter were gleaned from Brinkley's *American History;* Russell Freedman's *Franklin Delano Roosevelt* (New York: Clarion, 1990); William E. Leuchtenburg's *Franklin D. Roosevelt and the New Deal* (New York: Harper, 1963); and *The Encyclopedia of American History,* edited by Jeffrey B. Morris and Richard B. Morris (New York: HarperCollins, 1996).

OF FURTHER INTEREST

BOOKS

Freedman, Russell. *Franklin Delano Roosevelt* (New York: Clarion, 1990).

Hess, Karen. *Out of the Dust* (New York: Scholastic Press, 1977).

McCarthur, Debra. *The Dust Bowl and the Depression in American History* (Berkeley Heights, N.J.: Enslow Publishers, 2002).

Meltzer, Milton. *Driven from the Land: The Story of the Dust Bowl* (New York: Benchmark, 2000).

Partridge, Elizabeth. *This Land Was Made for You and Me: The Life and Songs of Woody Guthrie* (New York: Viking, 2002).

Stanley, Jeff. *Children of the Dust Bowl: The True Story of the School at Weedpatch Camp* (New York: Crown Publishing, 1993).

Steinbeck, John. *The Grapes of Wrath* (New York: Penquin, 2002).

Of Further Interest

Video and Internet Resources

The Plow That Broke the Plains. The classic documentary film by Pares Lorentz, made in 1937 for the Farm Security Administration.

The Grapes of Wrath. The 1940 film, directed by John Ford and starring Henry Fonda and Jane Darwell.

Voices from the Dust Bowl. American Folk Life Center, Library of Congress, http://memory.loc.gov/ammem/afctshtml/tshome.html.

Surviving the Dust Bowl. The American Experience, http://www.pbs.org/wgbh/amex/dustbowl/.

The Great Depression, the New Deal, and the Roosevelt Administration. The New Deal Network, http://newdeal.feri.org/.

Worth a Visit

The National Steinbeck Center, One Main Street, Salinas, CA 93901, http://www.steinbeck.org/MainFrame.html.

Dorothea Lange Collection, Oakland Museum of California, 1000 Oak Street, Oakland, CA 94607, http://www.museumca.org/global/art/collections_dorothea_lange.html.

Index

Note: Page numbers in **bold** type refer to illustrations.

Agricultural Adjustment Act
     (AAA), 32–33, 35
animals, deaths of, 20, **21**
Arvin Sanitary Camp
     ("Weedpatch"), 2, **3**
asparagus, harvesting, 50
Atlantic Monthly, The, 19
automobiles:
     belongings packed on, 1, **1, 36,**
          41–42, **42, 49**
     broken down, 43, 45, **45**
     on the road, 41–43, **43,** 45
     as shelter, **58**

barber, **53**
"black blizzards," **10,** 13, **14,**
          24–25, **25, 26**

"Black Tuesday," 17–18
Bound for Glory (Guthrie), 12
"bum blockades," 8

Caddo, Oklahoma, **30**
California:
     advertisements for workers in,
          48–49, **48**
     Imperial Valley in, 49
     labor unions in, 2–3, 5–6
     map, **44**
     migrant camps in, 3–5, **3, 4, 5,**
          46, 51, **51,** 52, 54, **56, 58,**
          59, 62
     migrant workers in, 1, **46,**
          47–55, **50,** 59–60, **60, 61,**
          62–63, 65–66

California (*cont.*)
  "Okies" fleeing to, 1–9, **1, 3, 4, 5, 7, 9,** 35, 37–45
  ranchers in, 47
  residency requirement in, 63
  on the road to, 38–45, **39, 40, 43, 44, 45, 49**
  Sacramento Valley in, 49
  Salinas Valley in, 49
  San Joaquin Valley in, 1–2, 5, 37–38, 45, 47, 49, 57, 65
  welfare funds in, 63
  winter in, **56,** 57–59
California Citizens Association, 60, 62
children, **46, 54, 55**
  dying of malnutrition, 4–5, 54, 57, 59
  haircuts for, **53**
  schooling of, 51–52, **52,** 55
Cimarron County, Oklahoma, 30
Civilian Conservation Corps (CCC), 66–67
Collins, Tom, 2, **3,** 58
conservation programs, 67–69, **70**
cotton picking, **48,** 49–50
cotton plantations, 35

Davis, James E., 8
disease, 52, 54

disk harrow, 15
Dust Bowl:
  area of, 14
  causes of, 15–16
  and conservation, 67–68
  description of life in, 19
  laws encouraged by, 69
  name of, 12
  out-of-work farmers in, 48–49
  Steinbeck's book about, 63
dust pneumonia, 25
dust storms, **10,** 11–15, **14,** 20, **22,** 23–32, **25, 26,** 32, 37

farms:
  abandoned, **20, 24,** 27–28, **28, 29, 31**
  conservation on, 67–68, **70**
  drought ended on, 66, **68**
  fair prices regulated for, 69
  foreclosures on, 28–29
  sharecroppers on, 35
Farm Security Administration (FSA), 2, 57
First Hundred Days, 32, **33**
Ford, John, 63
foreclosure, 28–29
freight trains, riding, 38–39, **40**

gas masks, 25–26

Geiger, Robert, 12
government, aid from, 68–69
Grapes of Wrath, The (movie),
   62
Grapes of Wrath, The (Steinbeck),
   63
Great Depression, 15, 16–17, 23
   bank closures in, 31
   city life in, 31–32
   description of life in, 19
   end of, 65–69
   homelessness in, 18, 32
   laws encouraged by, 69
   and New Deal, 32–35, 68–69
   unemployment in, 18, **19,** 48
Great Dust Storm (1935), **10,**
   11–15, **14**
"Great Dust Storm, The" (Guthrie),
   12
Great Plains:
   area of, 13
   depression in, 18, **19,** 23
   dust storms in, **10,** 11–15, **14,**
     22, 23–32
   native grasses of, 15–16
   rain returning to, **68**
   wheat crops in, 15, **16,** 18
Great Plow Up, 15
Guthrie, Woody, 8–9, 11–12, 37,
   38–39

Haggard, Flossie and Jim, 41–43,
   45
Henderson, Caroline, **27**
   and end of Dust Bowl, 66
   writings of, 19–21, 23, 27–28,
     29
Henderson, Will, 19, **27,** 66
homeless people, 18, 32, 57–59,
   59
Hoover, Herbert, 32

illness, 52, 54
immigrant laborers, 47–48
Indigent Act (1933), 62–63
In Dubious Battle (Steinbeck), 1

King, Lila Lee, 11

labor unions, 2–3, 5–6
lice, 52
Los Angeles, California, 8

MacManus, Thomas W., 59–60
malnutrition, 4–5, 54, 57, 59
martial law, 6
Mexican laborers, 47–48, **50**
minimum wage laws, 69
Model T cars, 41
Mojave Desert, 43, **45**
Morris, Jewell and Gladys, 41, 45

New Deal, 32–35, **33, 34,** 66–69

"Okies," 1–9, **1, 3, 4, 5, 7, 9,**
    37–45, **39, 55, 58**
    prejudice against, 6, 8–9,
       59–60, **61,** 62–63
    reasons for moving, 1, 35,
       37–38
    starvation of, 4–5, 18, 57, 59
"Okievilles," 3–5, **3, 4, 5,** 51, **51**
Otis, Elizabeth, 57

Pacific Rural Press, 8
Pearl Harbor, bombing of, 65
pickers, 47, **48,** 49–51, **50**
prairie grass, 15–16
prosperity, 15–17, 18

Rich, William, 63
"Roaring Twenties," 17
Robertson, Flora, 38
Robinson, Bill, 55
Robinson, Harold, 57
Rogers, Wayne, 52
Roosevelt, Franklin D, 32, **33,**
    67

Salinas, California, 5–6
Salvation Army, 57
San Francisco News, 1

schools, 51–52, **52,** 55
sharecroppers, 35
Shelter Belt, 67
sickness, 52, 54
Social Security Act (1935), 69
social welfare, 32, 63, 68–69
Soil Conservation Service, 67
squatter camps, 3–5, **3, 4, 5,** 31–32
starvation, death from, 4–5, 18,
    57, 59
State Relief Administration
    (California), 63
Steinbeck, Carol, 63
Steinbeck, John, **2,** 69
    as author, 1, 51, 52, 63
    "Pie Wagon" of, 1, 58
    travels of, 1–6, 57–59
stock market:
    crash of, 17–18
    investment in, 17, 69

tenant farmers, 35
Tortilla Flat (Steinbeck), 1
tractors, 15, **17,** 35
trees, planting of, 67, **70**
Tugwell, Rexford, 14
Turner, Roy, 31

unemployment, 8, 18, **19,** 48
unions, 2–3, 5–6

welfare funds, 32, 63

wheat:

    planting, 15, **16,** 18, 66

    reducing amount grown,
      32–33

"Why We Come to California"
    (Robertson), 38

Woodin, William H., **33**

working conditions, laws about,
    69

Works Progress Administration
    (WPA), 32, **34,** 35, 68–69

World War II:

    depression ended by, 65–69

    factory jobs in, **66, 67**

    Japanese American citizens in,
      65

    New Deal and, 66–69

    Pearl Harbor bombed in, 65

    soldiers in, **64**

About the Author

Michael L. Cooper is the author of over a dozen books for young adults on various aspects of American history. His most recent book, *Remembering Manzanar,* received the Carter G. Woodson Book Award from the National Council for the Social Studies. He lives in Washington, D.C.